CP Warrior

Jennifer Lee Vegas

Copyright © 2018 Jennifer Lee Vegas

All rights reserved. No part(s) of this book may be reproduced, distributed or transmitted in any form, or by any means, or stored in a database or retrieval systems without prior expressed written permission of the author of this book.

ISBN: 978-1-5356-1462-7

CP Warrior is a book about a thirteen-year-old boy named Joshua Xavier who discovers there's more to life than just CP.

Hi, my name is Jennifer Vegas and I'm Joshua's mom. I am here to share our story of how we have been overcoming CP, how having faith has a lot to do with it, and how having that strong family foundation also plays its part in the recovery.

I'd like to dedicate this book to my son Joshua for inspiring me to write it. Although there were rough days when I couldn't write, and some days I had to find some me time to write, when you read this book in its entirety, you will see why I say Joshua is very inspiring.

I'd like to know that I could help others living with cerebral palsy. Therefore, I wrote this book, to give others hope and a little support and to also let them know that there are resources out there. I hope this book helps those that don't have knowledge of cerebral palsy, Dandy-Walker syndrome, and autism, because these debilitating diseases make for a very long journey.

And I'm ready to share our journey with you.

Contents

Chapter 1 1

Chapter 2 15

Chapter 3 23

Chapter 4 31

Chapter 5 37

Chapter 6 47

Chapter 7 55

Chapter 8 63

Chapter 1

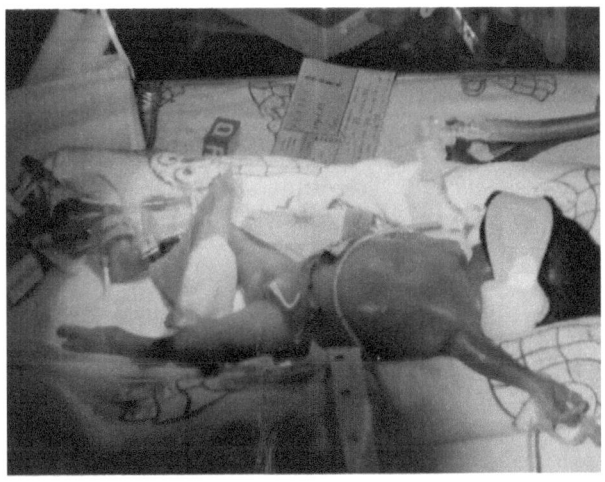

August 25, 2003. I had been going through three of the most excruciating hours of my life. I was only 24 3/7 weeks pregnant, and the doctors were trying their hardest to stop my contractions, but nothing seemed to be working. They gave me two shots of a medication for my baby's lungs to mature. They decided I had to be transferred to a hospital where they had a level-3 nursery. So, they chose University of Chicago Hospital, which has one of the best NICUs in the state of Illinois.

I was so worried, because I had lost two babies prior to this pregnancy due to complications of carrying to full term. They were both born at twenty-one weeks. So, one can understand why I was so worried! Not knowing if I was going to have to bury another baby was starting to take its toll on me. So, I started to pray the Lord's Prayer. And that kind of calmed me.

I was about ready to be transferred when my husband arrived. He had a look of concern on his face, but he still tried to console me. We didn't say much to each other; we just looked at each other. This was going to be his first living child. He was as scared as I was. Minutes later the paramedics arrived; it was already 5:00 a.m. The ride was going to be about thirty to forty-five minutes. My husband couldn't ride with us, so he had to meet us there.

As they put me in the ambulance all I could think was, "Please, Lord, save my baby; please don't take him from me; please give him strength!" I remember the feeling of ease coming over me. But then the ride started to get bumpy. And my contractions started to become worse and closer together. So, I started to get nervous as we approached the hospital. My husband was not there yet; he was still on his way. They took me to the labor room, and I was starting to get nervous because my husband was not there yet. My contractions were getting closer, and I hoped that I wouldn't have him without my husband here.

Three doctors, a nurse, and a nurse practitioner came into the room. The doctor explained to me that they had all the equipment here to keep him alive. He also said that the baby just made the viable mark, and that technology had changed drastically since I'd lost my last baby. So that gave me a little more hope.

Thirty minutes later, my husband arrived. The doctors had just got done examining me, and now it was time to discuss the good and the bad outcomes of having a preemie. They told me that when he came out into this world he would have to be intubated (they would have to put a tube down his tiny little throat, so he could breathe through a machine). So, my husband and I looked at each other and took a deep breath. All we could do was leave it in God's hands. All that mattered was that I made that viable mark! We had faith that everything would be okay.

It was almost shift change, and there was no one in the room with me. My husband went outside for some fresh air. The doctors were at the nurse's station along with the nurses. Last time they checked me I was seven centimeters, and that was when they had all left the room, about twenty minutes ago.

At 8:15 a.m. the nurse came in the room and I told her that I was feeling I must push. She told me, "Bad timing! It's shift change, what perfect timing the baby has." So, she checked me and walked out of the room and suddenly about twelve doctors and nurses practitioners ran into this tiny little room, pinning my husband against the wall, all to find out my baby's head was about to come out. We never made it to the delivery room. My poor husband was pinned against the wall looking like he was going to pass out. I had to coach him to breathe, all the while pushing our baby boy out. It all happened so fast. He was here. All I could wonder was what his cry was going to sound like! Then there it was… he sounded like a kitten. As they were putting him in the warmer I saw his arm rise, like he was trying to tell me, "Mom, I'm okay, I'm okay!" I gave a huge sigh of relief. Then the crying stopped. That was because they had to intubate him. I was just happy he survived. God heard my prayers.

They then rushed him to the NICU, so they could work on him, because he was in critical condition, being born at five and a half months. A lot of things were going through my mind at that moment. Like, what are they going to do with him? And how bad is the outcome? But then I remembered something amazing that had happened to me in church two months prior. I had just gotten baptized, and we were in the post-baptismal room with the minister. He asked us to close our eyes and pray. Mind you, there were at least twenty people in the room. So, I closed my eyes and lifted my hands in the air and started to pray and tears started to flow down my face. No one knew of my pregnancy – only my husband and me. So, then I felt a hand on my belly and I opened my eyes and the minister was standing there saying, "God told me to tell you, he will be okay!"

I said, "What!"

He said it again, touching my belly: "God told me to tell you he will be okay!" He then walked away from me. I was in total shock! I didn't know what I was having. Nor had I told this man I was pregnant. So that was the day my faith was built! And so that was why now, sitting in this room waiting to see my baby, I shouldn't worry or question what God had just done for us. This was a miracle! He was right; my baby was going to be fine! God was giving him all the strength he needed right now. I had faith that everything would be all right. God had sent His angels to help our little boy. He would pull through this long, tough road. Amen!

I remember the doctors coming back from the NICU to update me on the status of my baby. They said he was stable for now. I asked if I could go and see my son and the doctor said as soon as the nurses finished cleaning me up, my husband and I could go and see him.

When we arrived in the NICU, I saw these incubators aligned in a circle and two in the middle with one empty, waiting for my baby. At that moment, he was in a private triage room with the nurse. She was putting IVs in him. As we entered the room we saw a beautiful soft-toned-skinned, hazel-eyed, brown-haired woman who spoke with a soft tone. Sher was her name. I came next to my baby boy and grabbed on to his tiny, tiny little hand, and he grabbed on tight to my pinky finger. So tight that his whole hand turned white. At that point, we decided to name our son Joshua and nickname him Superman.

He already had three IVs in him, and she needed to put one more in. She was having trouble finding another vein, so she had to put it on his tiny little foot. I was just so happy to see Joshua being taken care of and that he was breathing, even though he had the respirator. I was very hopeful. I continued to pray to God to please make Joshua strong enough to live! I remembered to hold on to my faith in Him and not let go.

It was time for me to go back to my room, so I kissed my baby on his tiny head and whispered, "Mommy loves you and so does God!" When I came back to my room there were some nurses and my doctor talking.

They then came into my room and said, "We are here because we want to discuss a study we are doing called the ELGAN Study. We would like to know if you would like to participate?"

They explained to me that they take a piece of the placenta and some amniotic fluid from the birthing process (which had already been taken), test it along with other patients', and somehow link it to preterm labor. What they looked for was bacterial vaginosis. So, I agreed! And Joshua and I became a part of a huge study.

The next morning the pediatrician came in the room with a look of concern on his face to talk to me about Joshua. I asked him if everything was okay. He said he had some bad news. My heart dropped to the ground! I was alone; my husband had gone home to send my two daughters, Melissa and Bianca, to school. I wasn't ready to take in bad news all by myself! The doctor said he wanted to run some tests on Joshua's brain and abdomen, because Joshua had been having seizures back to back and he also had bleeding in his abdomen. So, they asked me to sign some consents for a blood transfusion so that they could start the transfusion on him. And he was also on some medicine for his blood pressure and his seizures. I just wanted him to get better. I wanted to hold him so badly. But I couldn't; there were wires, and they were everywhere. He even had a feeding tube in his belly button.

I called my husband right away and told him the news. He was heartbroken! He rushed right back to the hospital to be by Joshua's side. As soon as he arrived in the NICU the doctors approached us and asked us to go with them to a private room to talk to them about Joshua's results. So, they broke the news to us that Joshua had a grade-3 hemorrhage in his brain and a grade-2 hemorrhage in his abdomen. They said we shouldn't expect him to survive past the night. We were shocked by the news. I started to cry, and my husband grabbed me and hugged me and said, "Don't worry."

The first three nights were miserable because that was all we heard from the doctors: that Joshua wasn't going to live. But we held on to our faith. And chose not to listen to the doctors anymore. We knew he was a fighter; we knew he was going to live! No matter what the doctors said. We still believed in God's unconditional love and healing. We just knew he wasn't going to let us down. Not this time! And he survived. He heard our prayers.

You see, when you have faith in God, all things are possible!

Little did I know that Minister Greer worked at the University of Chicago Hospital as a radiologist/ultrasound technician. He was one of the techs that performed the brain and abdomen scans on Joshua. He did not know who Joshua's parents were. That was, until one day he came into the NICU and saw us by Joshua…and was in awe! He congratulated us and had one request, and that was that we'd give him permission to pray over Joshua that and every single moment he was in the NICU or at work. We all agreed, and the doctors agreed as well, because he wasn't family. He was our minister. Joshua was baptized right then and there. Right at that moment he was given more strength; the next day they did another brain scan and noticed that the bleed had stopped.

I'll never forget the feeling I had when we got the news that the bleeds were both gone; they were dissipating. This was evidence that God works when we least expect it.

When we were in the NICU we tried to stay positive, but there are times when we just felt hopeless, because we saw our baby lying there with machines all hooked up to him. They were on each arm and leg, and there was a feeding tube in his umbilical cord. He was tiny, weighing one pound, eight and half ounces, and only twelve inches long. He fit in the palm of my hand. All we could do was stay positive for him and us. We would look around the NICU and see all the parents crying and looking sad. I would try to talk to them to try to stay positive. There were all different conditions these babies were in. It was very sad. They saw how we would talk and sing to Joshua and how it would soothe him, and his heart rate would go up. He started to improve every day until he graduated, seventy-six days later. He went home without an oxygen tank or any other machines. The doctors said that preemie babies usually go home on oxygen. He only went home on two meds, For his seizures. He was a warrior of God! Yet we still had a long road ahead of us.

The doctors told us to be prepared for the worst! Like Cerebral palsy, developmental delay – they even said Joshua would never walk or talk. That he would never be "normal." The exact words the doctor and the nurse practitioner said to us were: "Don't expect much." These were words I didn't want to take in. I wanted to hear positive words.

Joshua needed to be enrolled into EeEarly Interventions. He already qualified for social security disability due to his birth weight, which he had started receiving while in the NICU. But all I could do was ask God for guidance, peace of mind, and strength for me and my family. Especially my two daughters, Melissa and Bianca. They were both asking a lot of questions that I didn't have the answers to. So, I often found myself turning to God for those answers. And He showed me the answers little by little daily. I would juggle all the appointments and errands on top of working full time. I often wondered how I did it every day. But then I remembered that it was all about my kids!

I had started a new job as a patient care technician in the mother/baby unit at McNeal Hospital in Berwyn, Illinois, while Joshua was still in the NICU. I wanted to learn more about how to take care of the sick. My heart was yearning for education. My job was convenient for me because it was across the street from the house. It was very easy for us as a family. To know that we had access to an ER so close to home was like a breath of fresh air. It was my job and somewhere he could go to be healed for anything that ailed my kids. With Joshua's epilepsy, I had to be close. My husband also worked nearby at a tire and lube shop about five blocks away. We both worked opposite shifts so that one of us was always home with

Joshua and the girls. It was hard because we barely saw each there, only on our days off. But we still stood strong!

At the age of three months Joshua was diagnosed with ROP, which is retinopathy of prematurity, a potentially blinding eye disorder that primarily affects premature infants weighing about 2 ¾ pounds (1250 grams) or less that are before 31 weeks of gestation (a full-term pregnancy has a gestation of 38 to 42 weeks). The smaller a baby is at birth, the more likely that baby is to develop ROP. This disorder, which usually develops in both eyes, is one of the most common causes of visual loss in childhood and could lead to lifelong vision impairment and blindness. ROP was first diagnosed in 1942.

Joshua had two surgeries to correct it. By the time he was one he was wearing glasses – which he didn't like! He had to see the neuropathologist every month to make sure his vision was good, and his retinas were intact. We also had to see his neurologist monthly for his seizures and his development. Joshua was diagnosed with cerebral Palsy soon after he turned one. We were devastated, but ready! Prepared! The doctors had warned us. We asked the doctors what the prognosis was. They said to us that Joshua was not going to walk or talk. But there was one thing they didn't realize: Joshua was already saying "Momma" and "Daddy." So, we didn't say anything more. What could we say – we were shocked. We had known something was wrong, but we just didn't know what it was. Or maybe we did, and we were just in denial.

What is cerebral palsy?

Cerebral Palsy (CP) is a disorder that affects muscle tone, movement, and motor skills (the ability to move in a coordinated and purposeful way). CP is usually caused by brain damage that happens before or during a baby's birth, or during the first three to five years of a child's life. The brain damage also could lead to other health issues, including vision, hearing, speech problems, and learning disabilities. There is no cure for CP, but treatment, therapy, special equipment, and, in some cases, surgery can help kids who are living with the condition.

So, what next? We asked the doctor. He said, "I am going to refer Joshua out for therapies – physical, occupational, and speech. Set up the appointments and contact Early Interventions and let them know his diagnosis. And they will help you from there with any resources you and your family may need." So, we took his advice and made all the phone calls – of course, after we were able to get ourselves together.

Joshua's physical therapy started when he was one and a half years old. He really didn't like it; he cried every time he had it. But he had to do it twice a week. He also had speech therapy twice a week. He loved it; he was learning sign language, as we were, too. Occupational therapy followed as well. That he enjoyed because it had to do with playing with toys. There were a lot of things we were still getting used to, but it was starting to get easier. His therapy started to pay off! He was starting to commando crawl, and he was also sitting up, scooting around on his butt. All I could remember was what the doctors told us in the beginning: that Joshua wouldn't walk or talk. But we knew that he would one day! We had faith. Joshua was even able to eat table food by spoon. He ate everything; his favorite food was spaghettis and meatballs, and applesauce. He had a special high chair made for children with special needs and custom fitted, so as he grew, so did the chair. It was very nice, and adjustable. We also used it when we would give him haircuts. Which was one thing he always hated; maybe it was the sound of the clippers.

Chapter 2

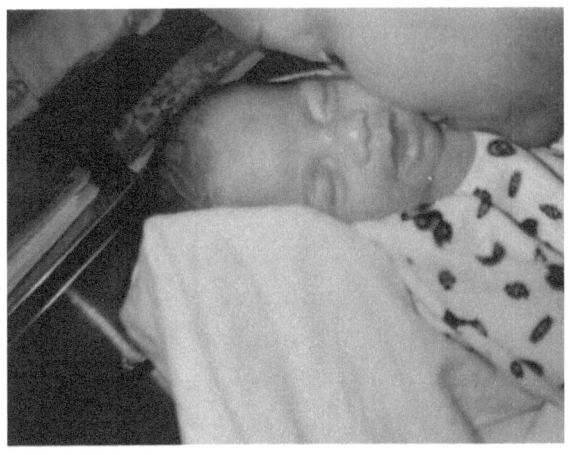

ONE DAY WE GOT A phone call from Sher, Joshua's NICU nurse. She wanted to visit Joshua. So, we planned a nice dinner at our house for the next day. When she arrived, she didn't come empty-handed. She had a gift for Joshua, Melissa, and Bianca. We were so happy to see her, not to mention so grateful for the gifts. The look on Joshua's face was priceless. It was like he had seen an angel. His eyes had this glimmer in them and his smile was from ear to ear. His legs were kicking, his arms were reaching out for her. I felt butterflies in my stomach when I saw him that way, because it made me feel so happy for him that he was feeling this way about her. She was his Guardian Angel for seventy-eight days. She was the one he opened his eyes for when he opened them for the first time, as his eyes had still been sealed shut when he was born for four more days. Sher had a soft voice, if you recall. That was what also drew him close to her.

She asked us how things were going. We told her that it was tough but that we were taking it a day at a time. That all we could do was pray and keep our faith. I told her that Joshua got therapy three times a week, plus his doctor's appointments were almost every week. It could be overwhelming, but all we could do was pray to God for guidance and strength. And that was what God had been giving us. Sher felt for us; she told us that she wanted to be there for us a little more. So, she said she would keep in touch with us, and that she did. She did it to relieve some stress out of our lives. Just being that shoulder to lean on, someone to run to that had the knowledge of babies born with illnesses. My daughters looked up to her. Sher would come over on occasion with her daughters to interact with my daughters while she spent time with Joshua. I could imagine how many lives she had touched and changed. I could only hope that I was not the only parent to come across her that felt this way about her. I hope and pray that she continues to help heal those babies in the NICU, for she is now a nurse practitioner. Since the last time I seen or spoke to her about six years ago, we've lost contact. I hope and pray that one day we meet again so Joshua can see her.

We were ready to celebrate Joshua's third birthday, so we threw him a party in the backyard and invited all our family and friends. Joshua was very excited. He had so much fun! He played with other kids that were there. He ate cake and ice cream. He walked a little in a regular baby walker and he did very well with that. He was walking with assistance. My husband and I were amazed at the progress Joshua was making despite what the doctors were saying or had said about his prognosis. He was about to transition from Early Interventions into pre-K that week, at Irving Elementary School in Berwyn, Illinois. It was a very good school; because my daughters were attending there. I was told their ESE program was good there, as well as their pre-K program.

So, we had an IEP scheduled for that week, and Open House to meet with the teachers and teacher's assistants. When we met with them they explained to us what they did daily. They explained to us how often Joshua would receive occupational, physical, developmental, and speech therapies. It was awesome that not only did he receive it at home, but he would also receive it at school.

Maryellen, Joshua's physical therapist, was the toughest lady in the nicest way. She was great with Joshua. She helped him to achieve his goals and milestones. She was there to help Joshua crawl, walk, and build his muscles. Especially his butt muscles. She would often say he had no butt, that we had to work on his butt muscles to help him walk. She had to work hard with Joshua because most of the time he would refuse to work with her. Maryellen grew an attachment to Joshua as soon as two months after working with him. He has a tendency of doing that to people. She said Joshua was stubborn but determined. She also would tell us it was Joshua's way or the highway! But she always had the ability to teach him what she needed to, per his goals. She was his therapist for seven years.

Joshua seemed to be progressing with his therapies. He was doing well in school, and he enjoyed being around his classmates. He had a best friend named Hailey. He lit up every time he saw her; he had to always be right next to her. The school had several fields trips every year that I would chaperone as well, like to the Shed Aquarium in downtown Chicago, or to the Brookfield Zoo in Brookfield, Illinois, which was Joshua's favorite place to go.

To see him progressing in the way that he was brought so much joy in my heart. I'd heard a story of a kid with CP whose parents would keep him confined in a room and not take him out anywhere, only feeding him PediaSure or milk, not giving him table food. I was so distraught over this. I cried the whole night about it, wishing there was something I could do about it. But I did pray about it. I knew somehow God was going to hear my prayer and help that poor child. We always treat Joshua like he is normal, so as he grows he can understand the concept of things and understand how life is.

When he was four we went to see his Neurologist at Loyola University Hospital's outpatient pediatric neurology department in Maywood, Illinois. They are a top-notch hospital. The doctor ran some tests on Joshua's brain, including an MRI. He had to be sedated for it, which made him a little loopy. He was cracking up laughing at everything. I think he was on cloud nine! Other times he would be kicking and screaming, but this day was a good day.

We had to return the following week for the results. When we returned for the results the doctor had a look of concern on his face. It wasn't looking good. He said to us as he was looking at the MRI that it revealed that the whole back side of Joshua's brain was all damaged from the bleed he'd had at birth. So, he performed a neurological exam on him from head to toe and diagnosed him with Dandy-Walker syndrome. Now, what is Dandy-Walker syndrome? Dandy-Walker syndrome is a congenital brain malformation involving the cerebellum (an area of the back of the brain that coordinates movement) and the fluid-filled spaces around it.

The doctor asked us if Joshua could be a part of a huge study with doctors from around the world. It was to take place in a week at Loyola Medical Center. Joshua would even get compensated for it, the doctor explained to us. His exact words were, "Joshua is going to make his first paycheck!" We agreed to have Joshua participate. He would be one of ten kids involved in the study. But he would be the main one. The rule was that we couldn't be in the auditorium with Joshua while they were doing the study; we could only be in the interview room. Joshua was little but determined to do things on his own. So, we knew he could do this study on his own.

On the day of the study Joshua was in such a good mood; it couldn't have been a better day to do it. Joshua was ready to GO! This was a HUGE moment for him, being in front of hundreds of doctors from around the world that were studying every movement Joshua made, how CP and Dandy-Walker syndrome affected the body. As they were in the auditorium, we were in the interview room answering questions about what Joshua could and couldn't do and at what age he accomplished his milestones. You see, there were a lot of things he couldn't do like a child that was born full-term and "normal." But he was doing things at his own pace. I think this was a real big learning lesson for us. There were lots of questions and tons of info for us. It was a lot to take in, but as parents of a special-needs child, you tend to learn how to take in all the info you receive. At times, it can get overwhelming, but just breathe and "let go and let God"!

When I say let go and Let God, I'm saying to let go of all your worries, all your stresses, and anything that is bringing you down. Hand it all over to God and ask him to take control of everything in your life. And you will see things starting to change.

With the support of my family – my mom, Margaret; my dad, Cesar; my brothers, Junior and Ramon; my daughters, Melissa and Bianca, my son Luis; and my sisters, Sandra, Malina, and Nicole – Joshua was able to start accomplishing his goals little by little. So, we knew Joshua was going to show the doctors differently than what we were told in the beginning. With God's grace and mercy, we knew he was going to walk and talk in a matter of time. My family tried to stay as positive as possible, because positive energy is good energy around a special-needs child. In the Bible, it says in 2 Corinthians, 5:7, "We walk by faith and not by sight." Which means when you have faith and believe in God and pray, nothing is impossible!

Chapter 3

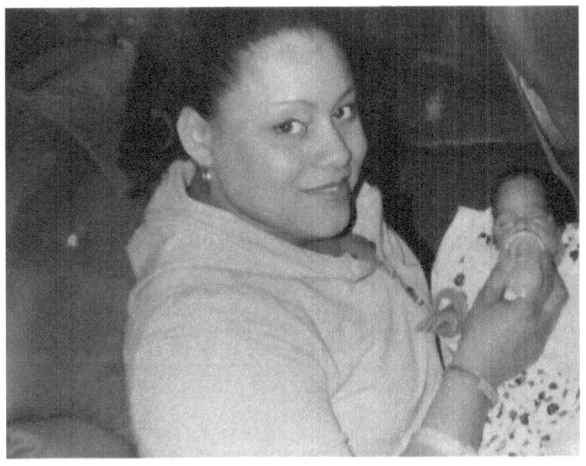

THAT SPRING MY BOSS HAD approached me and asked if I was interested in joining her department's group for the March of Dimes Walk America. I was elated and said yes! I felt that since the March of Dimes helped Joshua, I wanted to help other babies. So, I decided to recruit my mom and my sister Sandra. We had a large group of people. It was a 10k walk; my legs were so sore. But it was well worth it. I was really dedicated to finishing the walk. So, we did! We helped another baby…maybe even babies!

I said to myself that I was going to do this every year. The walk takes place in downtown Chicago at the Buckingham Fountain in Grant Park. It's a beautiful landmark in Chicago, Illinois. It's been there for decades. At the end of the walk they have a BBQ and goodies waiting for you at the finish line. So, yeah, it's well worth it.

I never knew how many programs and activities there were for special-needs children until after I did my first walk. I started to do some research on children with CP and found some interesting websites. I signed up on the Cerebral Palsy Network at CerebralPalsy.org. They are the ultimate resource for everything cerebral palsy for us.

I was even able to find respite care for Joshua. And our eldest daughter, Melissa, would get paid for babysitting Joshua for us while my husband and I would go and run our errands, or even go out on a date for a change, for some alone time. Those of you who are parents of a special-needs child know how hard it is to get some alone time. It can happen maybe once a month, and if you're lucky, maybe twice. But when you're away at those times the only thing that's on your mind is your child. Your mind and your heart are always on your child, 24/7. But you can't help it.

One day we were sitting at Schwab Rehabilitation Hospital in Chicago on Ogden Ave. and California Blvd. waiting on Dr. T., Joshua's orthopedic doctor. We had been seeing her monthly for about two years to see how good Joshua's gait and strength was and how well he walked with assistance. And he did well.

We then asked her, "When do you expect Joshua to walk?"

She said, "If he doesn't walk by the time he turns seven years old, I'm afraid to tell you that he will never walk!" She didn't think he'd be walking at all. But we still held on to that faith we'd always had. We stood positive no matter what. We said Joshua would do it at his own pace and in his own time, like he did with everything else. He already had his gait trainer (walker) to help him walk with assistance. So, we knew Joshua was very determined.

We'd seen numerous children with CP confined to a wheelchair, not able to do anything at all, and it broke my heart to see them like that. I prayed for them and their parents and families, and I thanked God for continuing to help my josh fight his battles each day.

Joshua was able to do a lot of things already. But by the time he reached seven years old he still wasn't walking. So, I decided to go and read my women's study Bible that had been given to me years ago by a pastor. I just felt the need to sit down and spend some time with God and feed my soul with his knowledge and his word to remind me that he is God and he would answer my prayer in due time. I just had to be patient.

In the Book of Matthew, 8:5–13, it says:

When Jesus had entered Capernaum, a centurion came to him, asking for help. "Lord," he said, "my servant lies at home paralyzed, suffering terribly." Jesus said to him, "Shall I come and heal him?" The centurion replied, "Lord, I do not deserve to have you come under my roof. But just say the word, and my servant will be healed. For I myself am a man under authority, with soldiers under me. I tell this one, 'Go,' and he comes. I say to my servant, 'Do this; and he does it." When Jesus heard this, he was amazed and said to those following him, "truly I tell you, I have not found anyone in Israel with such great faith.

This was what made our faith stronger as a family. So, I prayed even harder. I grabbed Joshua and hugged him as I was praying and asking God to please heal him and help him walk, and to help him talk and be as normal as possible. So little by little Joshua was starting to show progress. He was sitting up straighter, crawling a lot better, skootching around on his butt all over the house, and using his gait trainer. We were so proud of him and his accomplishments. I can thank his physical therapist from school, Maryellen, because she had been working so hard with Joshua all these years. She's the best I have met in Berwyn, Illinois, let alone Chicago! I would recommend her to anyone if I knew where she was now.

Joshua's godmother, Serena was even amazed at the things he has been able to do. Serena has been there for him since day one. She has always been a part of our support system. She would come with us to the NICU to see Josh; she adored her little Superman. She loves him so much she would do anything for him. She would give us much-needed advice, so we wouldn't feel alone. She was our shoulder to cry on when things got too tough for us. If we needed a break, she was always there. You always need that one person there for you when you're going through the ups and downs of cerebral palsy.

I also had my best friend, who is also my daughter Melissa's godmother, Silvia. We have been best friends for over twenty years. She has watched Joshua grow from the tiniest baby to pushing him to walk and talk. She would take my daughters, so we could have a break from time to time. She was also my support system, my family, my shoulder to cry on, my consoler. I want to thank both of you, Serena and Silvia, for being there for us, and for being a part of our family. We love you!

As we were walking home from picking up Joshua from school one day, there was an ambulance and fire truck driving past with sirens blasting. Joshua started to freak out and began to climb out of his wheelchair. I'd seen him freak out before, but not this bad. I felt so bad for him. I had to stop and take him out of the wheelchair and he was climbing all over me, scared. I was trying to console him. It took me about five minutes to calm him down. I couldn't understand what was happening to him.

The following morning, I discussed the incident with Joshua's teacher. She said she would discuss it with the IEP team that afternoon. Later that afternoon when I picked up Josh from school, there was a note/invitation in his bookbag for an IEP meeting for a re-evaluation and testing for sensory issues. It was scheduled for two weeks from then. So now I had two weeks to sit down and write down all the questions and concerns we had about Joshua.

Always, always – I cannot stress this enough – if you don't have an advocate at the meeting with you, please be prepared and write down questions and things you wish to discuss at your child's IEP meeting.

The day of Joshua's IEP meeting I was prepared. I had all my questions and concerns ready. I was told by the team that he needed more occupational therapy and developmental therapy. I was told it needed to be more intense; they were working on more goals with him. I asked them, "Will the noise issue he has ever go away?" I was told maybe, maybe not! In most cases with children who have CP it does not go away.

And so, I was concerned about this, as would any parent be. How were we going to get through this? I thought to myself, "We can only take it a day at a time and help soothe him through his attacks. It's just one more hurdle to jump over in the life of living with CP." So, as we went on with the meeting I was handed a paper that had info about support groups for parents of children with CP, which was something that was hard for us to do due to our work schedules. So instead I decided to do some online searching again and was directed to ChildMind.org, which is a very good resource for understanding sensory issues.

Chapter 4

As a parent of a child with special needs, you tend to forget to take care of yourself. Your health is of the utmost importance!

I found myself getting sick in the beginning of 2008. I was waking up in the mornings with temporary blindness lasting for about five minutes. I had very bad dizzy spells all day long, every day, and migraines every morning. I was seeing spots all day long; I felt so much pressure in my head and my eyes. One day my doctor sent me to see a neurologist. She couldn't find anything wrong with me but severe vertigo and prescribed me some Meclizine, which also causes dizziness, and it made me worse. So, she sent me to see a neurosurgeon.

That doctor was a lifesaver. The minute I walked in she looked in the back of my eyes and ran all types of tests on me, including a CAT scan. And in three hours I was diagnosed with pseudotumor cerebra (hydrocephalus). The doctor told me I could go blind, so she scheduled a spinal tap and put me on some Diamox to try to release the fluid from my brain. But after about six months of treatments it wasn't working, so she transferred me to another doctor at a different hospital, Loyola University Hospital's neurosurgery department.

I was very nervous when we first met with the doctor. He was so sweet and kind. He was the professor of the neurosurgery department, Dr. Vikram Prahbu. He went through the exam with me step by step, looked through my eyes, read my CAT scan results, and said to me that this was uncalled for! He told me that I needed surgery right away or that I could lose my vision. He said, "You have way too much fluid building up in your brain and in the back of your eyes – I will see you next week for surgery!" I was in shock! Me, brain surgery. I had Joshua and the girls to take care of! He set up a pre-op appointment to go over the procedure with me, so I could ask any questions.

After the appointment, I went home to discuss with Alberto, Melissa, and Bianca that I must have brain surgery, which is a delicate conversation to have with your husband and kids, because it is a sensitive part of the body that they are going to open. They were shocked and scared at the same time for me. I told them not to worry, that I would be much better after surgery. God would be with me; I had faith.

On the day of the pre-op appointment, my sisters Sandra and Nicole accompanied me for moral support and to ask questions. The doctor entered the room and introduced himself to my sisters and started to explain the procedure to us. They were going to place a VP shunt in my skull that connected to my brain and had a valve connected to it that went all the way to my stomach and continuously released the fluid through that valve into my abdomen. It was major surgery I was going to have in three days. I was very nervous. But all I could do was pray to God and ask him to cover me in the blood of Jesus. Amen! The recovery time at home was at least a month.

On the day of the surgery, I was still nervous, but I had done a lot of praying and my whole family was going to be there. I kissed my kids goodbye and hugged them tight and went on to the hospital. I was finally being taken care of after being sick for a year! As they were prepping me for surgery, my mom started to pray for me. I felt such a calm come over me; it felt good. I wasn't nervous anymore.

My surgery was supposed to take three hours, but it took five and a half hours. The first three hours was the doctors releasing the fluid from my brain. And the other two and a half hours was the placement of the VP shunt. I was in the ICU for four days and then put in a regular room on the neuro floor for two days, and then discharged home. It felt so weird to have a shunt in my head. It was like this hard device in my head that I could feel when the fluid was being transferred through the tube. But I did feel so much better! No more dizzy spells, no more blackouts, no more seeing spots, no more migraines! It was all gone! I felt less pressure in my head and in the back of my eyes.

All I could think about was that I must heal fast for Joshua and the girls. Melissa and Bianca were really worried about me. I couldn't imagine being teenage girls, having a little brother with CP and having to help with him, and now your mom is sick. Having to care for her and Joshua and the house while Dad was at work. They are great daughters and I can't thank them enough! They've done so much for Alberto, Joshua, and me. We thank you so much, girls, and we love you to the moon and back, TO INFINITY AND BEYOND!

As I continued to heal I would watch Joshua's progress every day. He was amazing; he would crawl to me and climb on me and say "Momma" and babble words. I barely understood him, but he was trying to talk to me and trying to take off my head wrap. But all I could do was smile and hug him and thank God for such an amazing child. It was like he knew something was wrong with me. It was then I knew I had to get stronger for my kids, so I could heal faster. My staples were to all be removed in a week, and I could go back to normal activities.

As Joshua got off me he fell and bumped his head. So, I reached over to pick him up and he looked at me like it didn't even faze him. He didn't even cry! I was afraid he would have a seizure. But he didn't…thank God! He hadn't had a seizure since he was two years old, and he was now seven years old. He had been on several anti-seizure meds since birth. Now he was just on one medication, Lamictal, and it had been controlling the seizures.

When the seizures first started while he was in the NICU, they were coming so often that they were uncontrollable with one medication, so he was put on several different ones. So, we were relieved and surprised that he'd lasted so long seizure-free! The doctors wanted Joshua to wear a special helmet, so he wouldn't hit his head anymore. But Joshua, being as stubborn as ever, would never wear anything on his head – hats, baseball caps, eyeglasses, or even the hood of his jacket or sweater. He wouldn't even wear gloves on his hands in the wintertime. So, we had to take extra precautions when it came to his head. Especially when he had a seizure. So, in all, helmets were out of the question!

Chapter 5

As Joshua grew through the next couple of years he continued to progress, although he still had his language barriers and physical limitations. We were still using his wheelchair and starting to use his walker a little more.

We did have a blessing when my granddaughter, Nevaeh, was born. She became Joshua's little sister, and his teacher. My daughter Melissa and Nevaeh lived with us, so we helped in raising her. While Melissa went to school we would babysit Nevaeh, so Melissa was able to attend massage therapy college to be able to give Joshua massages as a part of his therapies.

Little by little Joshua was growing a bond with Nevaeh. He gave her a nickname, "Lulu" – it was easier for him to say. So, it kind of grew on her. We all started to call her that. They played together a lot and watched cartoons together when he'd get home from school. She would crawl with him all over the place. She taught him how to crawl properly on his hands and his knees instead of commando crawling. And by the time Lulu was learning how to walk, Joshua started getting determined to try and take a few steps. We would get amazed at what he was doing, because he had endurance and determination. And it was his first time walking without assistance. Every day we started practicing with Lulu and Joshua in the living room and dining room to teach both how to walk. It was fun having to teach two babies how to walk. Although Joshua was not a baby physically, it was like teaching a baby how to walk for the first time. Joshua was still learning how to walk, but with patience and prayer he would be walking someday.

So, don't get discouraged if your child is not walking yet. It will happen on their own timing. Which was what Joshua was showing us. He was taking his time; he was not in a RUSH! Not yet! He would walk with us while holding our hands. He really didn't use his gait trainer in the house due to limited space. We tried to do as much practice as possible with the little equipment we had. Every little step Joshua would make was a miracle to us.

And it put a lot of hope in our hearts that one day he would be walking.

Never underestimate the glorious power of GOD! He has shown us that he is healing Joshua in a way that no man could do! He has also healed our family!

By the time Joshua turned eight years old the physical therapist from his school told us not to send him to school with his gait trainer because he didn't need it anymore. So, we kept it home to continue to teach him to walk without assistance. The therapist was super happy because he was starting to reach his goals. She had said that it was a matter of time before he took off walking. He seemed determined to walk; he would try every single day to walk. No matter how many times he fell, he would dust himself off like nothing happened and start all over again. Like nothing happened! Not a tear in his eyes! I could only imagine how he felt trying to learn how to walk. It must have been frustrating.

One day Joshua walked from the living room to the kitchen while I was cooking. By this time, he was nine years old. I must have almost burnt myself…I was so shocked! Our little boy was finally walking!!! We were so excited! All I could think and say was, "THE DOCTORS WERE WRONG!" He was really walking! He was overcoming CP! Praise GOD…THANK YOU, JESUS!!!

So, I tell you this: NEVER GIVE UP HOPE, NEVER GIVE UP FAITH, AND NEVER GIVE UP PRAYING! Because all things are possible through Christ. Remember to LET GO AND LET GOD!

Now that Joshua was walking we had to focus on his verbal skills and daily living skills. And then we could start proving to the doctors they were wrong all along, and that only God had control of what the outcome would be. Although most doctors have great skills, God still has control of everything. I see doctors as angels doing the works of God, like healing people. They cannot promise you a good or bad outcome. It all depends on what God wants for you.

Our kids are also angels in disguise. They tend to make us want to live a little more, hope a little more, and LOVE a whole LOT more. We've got to remember that they too have feelings of hope, life, love. That they to want to share, but sometimes it's just too hard for them to express their feelings. So, they tend to get mad and frustrated. Because they can't speak (being non-verbal). So, they tend to show their feelings in another way, most of the time with anger.

You must be prepared for it! Which means you must have the utmost patience with your child. I can count with both hand how many times Joshua had bad tantrums and started kicking and screaming, biting me and banging his head on things. And even head-butting me. His head is like a rock! And it hurt both physically and emotionally, because we can't do anything but talk to him to calm him down. We never used restraints on him or restrained him. We are 100% against it! Because it's so traumatizing for them, and they will also learn to dislike you and not want to be around you. I don't even agree with school or daycares using restraints on special-needs kids, because I've seen my share of news briefs on special-needs kids who died because of being restrained.

One morning Joshua didn't want to go to school. He threw the biggest tantrum ever, saying, "No school, no school please!" At this time, he only spoke a few words and the rest were in sign language. Anyhow, he fought tooth and nail not to go to school, even crying so hard. So, we didn't send him. We asked him why he didn't want to go to school and he said to us, "He hit me."

We asked him, "Who?"

He said again, "He hit me!"

We were upset. But we couldn't really get it out of him because he was non-verbal. He kept hitting his hand on the top of his head and saying, "No school, no school!" The next thing we did was call his teacher and tell her what Joshua had said. She was shocked and said she would get on top of it right away and talk to her staff in the classroom as well as the bus driver. She got back to me later that day and said that although she was absent that day, the rest of her staff didn't see anything out of the ordinary. She had a substitute teacher that day.

As the next day came we gave it another try…and the same thing happened! He still didn't want to go to school. He fought us tooth and nail again. Kicking and screaming! So, we didn't force him. I thought to myself, "This is serious, something happened to our son and I have to find out what!"

What I decided to do was call the principle and set up a meeting with her for that afternoon. We ended up bringing Joshua with us, but he really didn't want to be there. He kept saying, "Go bye-bye." At that point his teacher walked in and he was happy to see her and calmed down. So, we all knew it wasn't her. Our next question was, who could it be? His teacher had mentioned that the substitute teacher and her assistants were in the classroom now. She suggested that we take Joshua to the classroom to see how he would react. We all agreed and went upstairs.

As soon as we went up the stairs Joshua started to freak out. As we got to the classroom and opened the door, the male assistant was standing right there, and Joshua was screaming at the top of his lungs. But then when he saw the substitute teacher he went berserk! So, we left the room and went back to the office to discuss with the principle what had just happened. Her suggestion was to interview each one of the staff members in the classroom and the bus driver on Joshua's last day of school. And that she would get back to me.

The following week she got back to us and said we needed to have a meeting to go over the investigation. We set it up for the following Wednesday, which was two days away. Waiting two days is like waiting a week when it comes to your child! In the meantime, we took Joshua to the doctor and were told to take him to the ER. The diagnosis was abuse and neglect per the signs he was showing. We were floored! What was going through my mind were a million and ten things I could do to whoever had done wrong to my child!

But then I heard a voice tell me, "He will be okay!" which brought me back to when Joshua was in my belly and Minister Greer had delivered that beautiful message to me. That was the moment I calmed down. I asked for strength and courage to go through this investigation with Josh as peacefully as possible so that he was at peace and didn't relive whatever it was that happened to him. We had to wait on the results of the investigation patiently. When the day of the investigation approached we weren't ready for what we were about to hear. But we had to listen closely. I remember having severe anxiety before going in there, so I prayed to God. As the RCS worker started to read the investigation report I took a deep breath and closed my eyes for a quick second.

It turned out that the substitute teacher had said she restrained our defenseless son by the torso all the way to the ground for not saying the words "I'm sorry." Which we all knew that Joshua was a non-verbal child and had never said those words before. The substitute teacher basically got caught in her lie! Now we had to deal with the fact that our son was traumatized by this incident. I was so hurt and floored at the same time. But I had to keep my composure. I wanted to start yelling but tears started to flow down my face. And when that happens I usually do start to yell, but God had full control of the situation.

I said, "What gives her the right to restrain my son all the way to the ground like that!"

They said that restraining a student was not in their "PROTOCOL." I told them that I was pressing charges on her.

We went to the police department to file charges on the substitute teacher. The investigation took about a month and was closed due to not enough evidence… what? She had confessed – what more evidence did they need?! So, long story short, the police department didn't do a proper investigation. We felt so bad for our son. What were we to do now? How was he going to get an education? The school kept pressing us about Joshua returning to their school. But he still refused. So, we went to the next school board meeting and brought up the incident, what the protocol was, and what the next step should be. We ended up getting kicked out of the meeting. We got nowhere and nowhere FAST! I don't understand why, when our children don't have a voice to speak up for themselves, some people choose not to listen. You will run into them from time to time.

I can't stress enough how IMPORTANT it is for us to be our child's voice. WE ARE THEIR ADVOCATE! So, we need to speak up for them. DO NOT GET DISCOURAGED when things get tough. That's when you should use your voice and be HEARD!

We – me, my husband, and the IEP team – came up with a good plan for Joshua to continue getting the best possible education. And that was to send Joshua to an all-special-needs academy located on the northwest side of Chicago. It was called Horizon Academy. Joshua was very eager to go there. He loved it there; he was with other students like him. He always had a huge smile on his face every day when he came home from school. It was a beautiful thing to see that he was comfortable, after the ordeal he had just been through. Horizon was very good to him. They were caring, loving, and made sure all his needs were met. And beyond! It was the first time in a long time I had seen Joshua so happy. You don't know the joy in our hearts we had. He was learning a lot of new things and eager to become independent. They would even have

Special Olympics for them, which he loved. They held all kinds of events for the students and families.

But, sadly, all of that had to end abruptly at the end of the school year. He was not returning for the following year due to the old school district not wanting to fund it anymore because we still lived in their district. So, we had no choice but to send him back. They had just built a new middle school, which he would be attending, with the same teacher and new teacher's assistants. We were also told that the substitute teacher that had restrained Joshua was not able to renew her contract with the school district. I was elated to hear that.

Chapter 6

JOSHUA ONLY ATTENDED THIS SCHOOL until April of 2014 because we had prepared for our big move to Florida, which was a very big step for us. We about to leave our family, the family Joshua had known his whole entire life including his sisters, Melissa, twenty-two, and Bianca, twenty-one, and his brother, Luis, nineteen, and also my mom, my dad, my brothers, Ramon and Junior, and my sisters, Sandra, Malina, and Nicole. These are who have had a major impact on Joshua's life.

The move was starting to impact Joshua's life before we even left. We didn't know how to handle it. But with God and prayer we were able to get through the packing and goodbyes.

On the way to Florida Joshua got to meet the pilot and go in the cockpit. He was able to sit in the pilot's seat and wear the hat and take pictures with him. He saw all the buttons everywhere and wanted to touch them. He was so excited, he didn't want to leave the cockpit. He loves planes. When we got to our seats Joshua wanted the window seat, so he could look out the window the whole flight; he didn't even want to take a nap.

As we arrived at our new state of residence I realized Chicago was no longer home. I was sad but happy at the same time. Sad because I'd left my children and family behind. Happy because we were starting a better, happier future for Joshua. I knew deep down inside it would be a long, tough road ahead, because Josh was going to miss his siblings. But my husband and I had to stick it out for the sake of Joshua's new life here.

The first 3 months were hard, especially for Joshua; he didn't want to leave the house at all! That was one of his favorite things to do. We felt so bad for him because he would just lie on the floor and look out the patio doors, and sometimes start crying out of nowhere. And since he was Non-Verbal we didn't know why he was feeling that way now. We would ask him, and he would just say, "I don't know." Or we would ask yes or no questions. But he still didn't want to communicate with us.

Not only did Joshua fall into a deep depression, but my husband and I did as well. We missed our kids and grandkids, and our family. We also had absolutely no furniture at all; our apartment was empty. All we had for the first three months was an air mattress and a TV – that alone can be depressing! Just looking at white walls all day long. That was, until we were blessed with a full house of furniture. It was donated to us. It made our apartment a lot livelier. We had downsized from a two-bedroom to a one-bedroom. FRESH START! Joshua was little by little breaking out of his shell.

As we were meeting new people and making new friends, Joshua started to become a little more secure. We started to search for support groups to meet with people just like us, who could relate with us, since we didn't have any of my family here. We also very much needed "ME TIME." We hadn't had that in a few years.

So, I found out about Nathaniel's Hope from Joshua's case manager, Jennifer M. She is great at finding everything we need for Joshua and for us as a family as well. Anyhow, Nathaniel's Hope is an organization that helps families with children with special needs to "BUDDY BREAKS" and other special events for the family. They are also a great resource to have. The website is **www.NathanielsHope.com**. When you just want to relieve some stress, or are overwhelmed, you and your spouse can go on a long-needed date or catch up on some errands while someone certified at a Nathaniel's Hope-affiliated church watches your child and does fun activities with them.

When we first moved here two and a half years ago, we didn't know where anything was. But when we met Jennifer M., she was a godsend! She connected us with all the resources for low-income families and people with disabilities. To this day she is still a dear friend of mine even though she is no longer Joshua's case manager. She always went above and beyond for our family.

Joshua also has a very good insurance plan here in Florida through Medicaid called CMS. They cover almost everything he needs medically. Some things may take a few months to cover, like a new wheelchair or walker. But they do cover it. They also cover his in-home therapy – physical, occupational, and speech – and respite care.

His physical therapist, Carolina Rincon, the owner and Founder of NuCare Therapy in Kissimmee, Florida, is very good… She also went above and beyond with Joshua. When she first started seeing Joshua two and a half years ago, he wasn't walking very well, and he had very bad balance and posture. He didn't know how to dress himself or put his shoes on. Now he's walking and running and dressing himself with some assistance. She did things with him that amazed me. Out of all his therapists, she showed so much commitment every week to take walks with him and me as a part of his therapy. And we would jog on the bike path to prep him for the Special Olympics in the track and field division. We play kickball with him, had him walk in a straight line, and played catch. Joshua grew on her pretty fast and she grew on him. He now asks for her every single day. He wakes up in the morning and she's the first name he asks for. "Where's Carolina?" She's like a part of the family. She loves Joshua so much, and he loves her too. She praises his every achievement, especially during therapy. He always gives her BEAR HUGS. REALLY TIGHT! And he is a very strong boy. Don't let his skinny little size fool you – he's got STRENGTH!

For half the school year of 2014 to 2016 Joshua had to be on Hospital/homebound schooling, because for some odd reason one morning in 2014 he got up and refused to go to school, which brought us back to the day of the incident back in Chicago. This continued for the next couple of weeks, until we decided to hold an IEP meeting. And another, then another, until we finally came up with what we thought was a great plan at the time.

In May of 2015 we decided to put Joshua on hospital/homebound schooling, which really didn't help him much. It set him back a lot, because he wasn't receiving all the services he qualified for through the McKay Scholarship that he had been receiving in school. He was struggling. But he was starting to trust people again. His teacher tried very hard with him because it was a struggle in the beginning with Joshua. But at the end Josh trusted him and engaged with him.

And we as parents stepped in and educated him as much as we could as well. We added the *Starfall* app on his tablet and phone – it's an educational app that has ABC's, mathematical, and picture games on there for kindergartners on up. It's a great app to have for them. You see, Joshua is a technology kid. He's very, very smart when you hand him a cellphone, tablet, Smart Board, or anything that's technology, he will learn how to operate it. He will make your jaw drop! He has made many people question me "how a kid with cerebral palsy learns how to use technology?" My answer is, it's ALL GOD! My advice to you is to give your child one of those devices and let them show you how great God is and let them AMAZE you with their capabilities. You would be surprised.

I keep imagining Joshua when he gets older working in the technology field. Like in IT, debugging things. That's how smart he is. Joshua has taught us knowledge and unconditional love and has given us strength every day and a reason to live life like there's no tomorrow. We never doubted God; He has shown us that he can fix a horrible situation and turn it into a BLESSED MIRACLE. Because that's what Joshua is: he's a miracle.

He is now a thirteen-year-old teenager in eighth grade. Wow, how time flies! He's almost as tall as I am and has a little peach-fuzz mustache on his face. He's growing into a little man – where's my little Josh going? He's starting to become a little more independent and do things on his own, like getting his own cup from the refrigerator, putting his toys away, keeping everything in order. The doctor says he has OCD. But they recently diagnosed him with autism spectrum disorder. He also was diagnosed with conduct disorder for the problems he was having in school, not getting along with the school staff.

This year he's exhibiting the same behaviors in school that he had the previous two years. So, I feel as if we are back to square one. So, in the meantime, while working with Joshua, transitioning him into school, we applied for the Step Up for Students scholarships and the McKay scholarship. We got approved right away, which meant we could look for a private school for him to go to. We found one, but the scholarship amount wasn't enough. So, we hired an advocate team that specialized in IEPs to have your child's score raised so that the scholarship amount goes higher. It took months, and by then Joshua had already gotten accustomed to the staff and students.

The IEP specialists helps you with knowing your and your child's rights; they are advocates here in the state of Florida. They can also help you fix any issue you have with your child's IEP. It is always a great idea to have an advocate with you at meetings, preferably one with a legal background. Then you'll begin to understand your and your child's rights much more clearly.

Chapter 7

Joshua had been having a little rough patch these past two and a half years, and that was because we left our entire life and family behind to start a whole fresh, new life with new people. And that is tough for any child, let alone one with cerebral palsy and autism.

Not only was it hard for him, but it was hard for us as a family. I thought to myself, "What did we just do? Did we make the right move? YES, YES, YES, WE DID! It's just a bump in the road, that's it. It will come to pass. WE'VE GOT THIS…GOD HAS GOT THIS! If CP hasn't taken us down, then this sure isn't going to take us down! Amen!!!" We had all the faith in the world that we would get through this, and we did.

Joshua has his grandparents from my husband's side out here. They don't really understand him very much, but they are spending as much time as they can with him to get to know and understand him better, since we lived in a different state all his life. We did visit a few times, as they visited us. But Joshua loves them dearly and asks for them daily. There's not one day that goes by that he doesn't ask for them. I know deep inside he misses our family, because I sure do. Bianca and Melissa visit from Chicago to spend time with us, which is great.

Often, I feel as if I don't do enough for him. But I devote all my time to him 24/7. I try to stay as strong as possible for him, but it gets a little overwhelming, and that's when I turn to Father God and start praying like I never prayed before, letting all the tears out, asking him for strength and guidance. And that he has given me! He guided me to write this book. I've never been so clear-minded in my life. You see, Joshua is thirteen years old now and he's growing before our eyes. And doing amazing things that we were told he would never be able to do. He makes me STRONG every day he keeps me going.

One day we received a phone call from my mother-in-law, Gina, regarding a dog a friend from her job was donating. It was a Chihuahua puppy. And she asked if we wanted it. We said yes right away because we had been looking for an emotional-support dog for Joshua and hadn't found one just yet. It was like God was hearing us! We were excited and wanted to surprise Joshua. And that we did.

The next day my husband, Josh, and I all went to go and pick up the dog. Joshua had an ear-to-ear grin on his face. We met the dog and he was so loving and jumped in the car like, "Hey, this is my new family!" And he adapted right away. So now Joshua has his very own emotional-support dog and he's house-trained. Joshua loves his dog very much; he even goes to take him for a walk and play catch.

We try to treat Joshua as normally as possible because he's fighting this tough sickness called cerebral palsy. Plus, he was recently diagnosed with autism spectrum disorder (ASD). For the past three years I had been noticing signs of autism in Joshua. I finally brought it up to the doctor. The reason I hadn't brought it up to the doctor before was because I thought all along these signs were all related to CP. As I researched…because that's what I love to do…I started to see that Joshua had significant signs of autism spectrum disorder. So, after speaking with the doctor and evaluating Joshua, he diagnosed him with ASD. We were prepared for it because we knew he had it all along. We just must continue to do what we've been doing all this time: praying and research. Research for the knowledge and to know what to pray for. So now he has two sicknesses he must fight every day. But I'm going to tell you this: our boy is S.T.R.O.N.G. He's a CP WARRIOR; he's a WARRIOR OF GOD! That's why we nicknamed him "Superman."

I can't imagine what he's going through day in and day out, having seizures in the middle of the night that last five minutes, or sometimes two minutes. And they are very strong ones. Those are very scary moments for us. But I must stay calm and strong for him. And the crazy thing is that when he comes out of his seizure he doesn't remember a thing and acts like nothing ever happened. The neurologist just had to increase the dosage on the medication for his seizures because after twelve years of being seizure-free he had a seizure while he was sleeping (sleep-induced seizure) that lasted more than five minutes. And the doctor said they came back because he's growing and he's going through puberty. They are back stronger than ever. So, we must watch him closely. And I'm praying to God that they go away again. Or just never come back.

God is curing my son little by little, and I believe that one day Joshua will be seizure free and walking as straight as possible and talking clearly. Because he's a very determined child of God, who says a prayer every night and thanks God for his every day, yes, he does!

At a recent PT appointment with Carolina Rincon, his therapist, she said we had to ditch his wheelchair and order a posture-rest walker with a seat on it so that when he gets tired of walking he can just sit. She said that he's doing very well and those are words we love to hear.

I also met Joshua's school physical therapist recently and she admired Joshua and his endurance. She said that he was very nice to her. He did everything she asked of him. She had asked me a few questions about his childhood development, so she'd know what she had to work with.

I was there picking him up early because he was having tantrums again. He didn't want to be there. This went on for the next few days. I would drop him off at 8:55 a.m. and halfway there he would stop the wheelchair on me several times. And we would have to turn around and go home because I was not going to hurt myself by forcing him to go to school; I already had hardware in my back. The school understood. What more could I do? I wasn't going to force him and continue to hurt myself.

"Oh, dear God, there must be something else we can do," I said. I did have major back surgery in 2010. As we turned around to go back home I noticed how calm he got right away. He was acting so normal, like nothing had happened. Oh well…I guess we will just keep trying every day. Somehow, he must get used to going back to school.

Each day became a struggle, but with progress. Each day became emotionally hard for me. But I had to do it. I had to be strong like I always have been. Don't lose faith. Don't lose courage. Seeing him cry and throw tantrums really broke my heart; I had to sneak away every time. But now this week he is doing better. Thank God! He's finally transitioning back into school. Although I have my back issues I put that to the side and fight the fight of CP with Joshua. He needs an education and that means pushing him to school, because he refuses to take the bus and he's not a light person.

The teacher says that he only cries for about five minutes after I leave. Then he's back to normal. He'll play on the Smart Board, go on the computer, do some schoolwork, do therapies, and go to gym. I think he just has separation anxiety. Because he's been on hospital/homebound schooling for over a year, he's used to being home with us. But now he's going to be around a teacher, two paras (teacher's aids), and four other students that really like Joshua. The class is even going on a weeks-long field trip to the YMCA for swimming lessons. That's awesome! Although Joshua doesn't like pools – he won't even step a foot in one – I'd like for them to try. I can't understand why he loves the beach but not pools. I just don't get it! The sand, the water…everything at the beach he absolutely LOVES! We have a pool where we live but don't utilize it because of Joshua. I really do hope that when they go to the YMCA it works out well.

The teacher told me to be expecting a call from the school psychiatrist because they must test Joshua themselves for ASD. It's a mandatory testing when they get a diagnosis from a doctor, since Joshua was diagnosed this past August. So, she called me the following day and asked me to come in to fill out two questionnaires about the things Joshua can and can't do. Things he does and doesn't do. It took about two hours to complete. Then when she was done with me she had to start testing Joshua in the school setting. And that was a two-day process. Now to wait for the results, which take about two months, she said. The school psychologist already told the teacher that she does see autistic characteristics in Joshua. I was also told that he did great on the testing.

Let me explain to you a little about autism spectrum disorder. It's very hard for people with ASD to be around large crowds/crowded places. Let me tell you, I've had my share of stares when Joshua would have his tantrums (episodes) about wanting to go bye-bye! They are also attached to a single object – trains, cars, a toy, a blanket. In Joshua's case it's his trains. He makes these movements in his hands with them. He also makes these odd movements with his head and babbles all day long. Children with ASD also won't look you in the eye. They have social behavior problems. Now, I am not am I a doctor, nor do I know all the signs of ASD, so please consult your doctor for information about it.

Children with ASD are very, very smart. Joshua is very intelligent. He may not know simple things like how to tie a shoe. But he sure knows a lot about technology. You give him a cell phone and he knows how to work it. You give him a tablet; he's good at that too… Put him in front of a Smart Board. He's a GENIUS! Sometimes I wonder if Joshua is going to be like that scientist Stephen Hawking who had ALS. If Stephen Hawking can do it, so can Joshua.

Joshua is going to be someone inspiring for people. I say that because he inspires us. And I know that he will touch the heart of others the same way he does ours and our loved ones'.

Chapter 8

As a baby, Joshua underwent two eye surgeries for ROP (retinopathy of prematurity) severe epilepsy, two surgeries for tubes in his ears to prevent ear infections, a tonsillectomy, and an adenoidectomy. And he stood strong and continued his fight. That made me even stronger. And all throughout this I had my four brain Surgeries in a five-year period for my shunt revisions. Like I said…Joshua, Melissa, Bianca, and my husband, Alberto, made me stronger each day. I never thought in a million years that God would've planned my life out the way it is now. I couldn't ask for it any other way. Because I've learned a lot all these adult years that I was too naïve to as a teenage mom.

Life was tough until we had Joshua. He kind of opened my eyes about the true meaning of love, life, and happiness. Oh, and let me not forget determination! That's why he's doing the things the doctors said he couldn't do.

Jennifer Lee Vegas

We entered Joshua into the Special Olympics because I knew he would succeed, as he does in everything else. He ran in the track and field division and won two first-place ribbons, one for track and one for field. He also played in the basketball division and won a second-place ribbon. Joshua's endurance level is at 100%. He always achieves his goals, in and out of school.

Joshua loves the Special Olympics. Carolina had prepped him for track and field. Thank you so much for your hard work, Carolina. I'm so happy that Joshua can do normal things now. He always seems super happy when he achieves something. Joshua is known as a "Go Getter" you tell him to do something and he will do it. And when he gets praises for it he gets super excited. He will put a huge smile on your face.

Like when it comes to his trains, when they're dumped all over the floor, I try to pick them up, but he always tells me, "No, Mom, I got this," and he'll pick it up for me. But when Daddy asks him to do it, he won't do it for Daddy. He also tries to dress himself and put his shoes on.

Joshua also knows his sense of direction. He would point out which way to walk as we would walk to school each morning. And as soon as we got to the school he would tell me, "Go, Mom," and walk away with the teacher. Little by little he is showing me he's not a child anymore. That he's a young man. And he's a very polite one at that! He has manners: he says please and thank you, and you're welcome.

Sometimes he reminds us of an old man. He goes out on our beautifully planted patio and sits in the cushioned chair to look at the forest behind our house. And it's beautiful, calming, and relaxing out there. And let me add therapeutic. He sits out there for about a half hour. And this is the same place where I sit and write this book. We see all kinds of tropical birds, and peacocks, blue and purple ones. I love that Joshua loves nature. Since we moved here that's all he ever does, go out and sit on the patio.

I sometimes wonder what goes through his mind while he sits out there, Because he's always in such a daze. He just stares at the trees and the sky. He looks so peaceful out there. I wonder if he thinks about what he is going through. All the good accomplishments he has done, maybe?! I wonder if he remembers a lot of things, the struggles?! Well, only he and God know. Joshua is a unique child. And all children with CP or any disability are unique in their own way. God makes them special and unique for us.

Let me explain it to you like this… God chooses parents that are special, some of whom are going through a tough time in life and puts these precious angel baby preemies in our lives to change us and teach us what true love is. We become better people and it's not about us anymore, it's about them. Emotionally, mentally. We look at life a whole lot differently now that we are caring for such a precious human being. We must be a lot gentler with them, but treat them as normally as possible, because they need to feel normal. They deserve that. It makes them feel good and independent. But also, be soft with them, because, remember, they do have special needs.

Joshua never liked being treated like a baby or anything other than normal. We honestly didn't have to be reminded of that. I think this is the reason he is accomplishing all his goals. One at a time!

With Josh being in school full time now, and my husband working overtime, I've been feeling a little lonely. But sometimes it feels good because I have some "me Time." Does that make me a bad mom? No! But it does sometimes. I know I shouldn't feel that way. But I can't help it. As soon as Joshua gets home I'm full of life again. People tell me it's okay to feel this way: happy because I'm finally alone; I can finally breathe and gather my thoughts at a decent pace.

I'm here to tell you that it's okay to feel this way. I mean, how else are you going to take care of you? I'm a CP mom…if I don't take care of myself, the DAD has to take care of Joshua AND me. So, go ahead and take that "me time" and breathe a little, gather your thoughts, and do something for you. And don't feel any guilt. Because you and your spouse are the glue in the family and things must get done. And for things to get done you have to be at your fullest attention and at your best! There are doctor's appointments, therapies, schools, etc., so you must be at your absolute best.

But don't forget about family time, either. You must make time for family night. That's important! Find some family things to do. Like go to the zoo or museum. Or go for a long walk at the lakefront and have a picnic. Or go out to the movies and dinner. Maybe the beach. Joshua loves the beach, so we try to make it out to the beach as much as possible. He loves the sand; he likes to test his balance on it. And he loves how it feels on his skin. Kids with CP love the way the sand feels on their skin. So, family time is extremely important as a part of a foundation for raising a child with CP and autism.

There are going to be things in life that are going to seem unfair that we cannot control. Like when people look at us strangely when our child acts out of control at the store or in public. Or makes loud noises and moves their head uncontrollably. And we can only try to control the situation as calmly as possible with a smile on our faces. Sometimes I feel as if I want to break down, but then I remember that I have God on my side. And little by little the stares stop, and the noises stop, and the situation is controlled. AHHHHH…I got this! God is so GOOD! After all these years you get used to the stares and whispers, but it still is an uncomfortable feeling.

Sometimes I wish I could put myself in my Joshua's shoes! Just once, so I can feel what he feels. I probably wouldn't make it one day in his shoes, just seeing what he goes through day in and day out. He's an amazing, enthusiastic child of God. He's a fighter; he takes what is given to him with pride. Daily, he has challenges I don't think any one of us could fight. And he's still fighting them! And still STANDING TALL!

"Joshua's fight will continue until he gets older" is what one person told me. I tell you something…that's not going to stop us from having faith that he will conquer CP. That he will be normal. That he will be able to live on his own one day when my husband and I are no longer here. Or maybe even get married. I mean, I would love for him to live with us forever. These are just a few of my ambitions for him one day.

Let me share something with you: the day Joshua ran in the Special Olympics, I cried while I recorded the event. Because he was doing something the doctor said he would never do. He laughed the whole way, he was so excited for what he was doing. Carolina Rincon was there with her family to support Joshua.

God gave Joshua the strength to run. Thank you, Jesus, for giving him more to do than expected. More than we ever thought he would do. I knew he wasn't alone; I knew God was by his side this whole time. I always look back at the poem "Footprints in the Sand," my favorite poem. Especially when it comes to Joshua.

> My precious, precious child.
> I love you and would never leave you.
> During your times of trial and suffering,
> When you see only one set of footprints,
> It was then that I carried you.
> – Your Heavenly Father

God never leaves our side! You see, never lose faith. My heart yearns for more of Joshua reaching his goals. But we can only take it one day at a time and be patient with him. Like we've been doing all this time.

Joshua did one of the most amazing things at school at the end of his eighth-grade year. I picked him up from school one day and his teacher said that he'd amazed her. The first thing was, one of the paras (teacher's aids) had asked Joshua in Spanish "Como estas?" and his response was "Estoy bien." Now, Joshua doesn't know how to speak Spanish. I said, "What…he said that for real in Spanish?" She said yes! He must be listening to their conversations and learning along the way. I was shocked.

The second thing was, the teacher had announced that there was going to be swimming lessons tomorrow, and Joshua said, "I'm not coming tomorrow!" I said, "Are you serious!" She said yes, nodding her head. This means my son is talking a lot more clearly now. And a lot more now to other people besides us. He's a very upfront kid.

We used to barely hear him speak. He's always making loud noises all day long, and from time to time asking for a snack or saying, "go bye-bye." But now he's starting to speak in complete sentences when asked something. Like he'll answer, "I don't want that" or "all done." He is now speaking for himself when he's not around us. For the first time in my life I feel a little more relief that Joshua is starting to speak for himself. Because you never know when he might have to use his voice one day to fend for himself from a bully. Thank God he hasn't bumped into one. Because we all know there are plenty of bullies out there, especially when it comes to people with special needs. And there are so many bullies in the school system that they can't even control. I just hope and pray that my son or any child with special needs never has to encounter a bully ever. Because it's the worst feeling ever.

Joshua has been through enough socializing; he's come a long way thanks to his therapist, Carmen Cruz, M.A., from Impower here in Florida. She really helped him overcome a lot of his social fears. He now is integrating little by little with other students. He's enjoying school again. And when I told her that he was back in school full time she was crying. Crying tears of joy. Because it was very hard for us to get him out of the house. He didn't want to go to school because, remember, he had that huge fear of going to school. My hairs are standing up right now as I speak about this because it was a very hard time for us to endure.

Joshua is now in high school, enjoying his freshman year with a GPA of 3.749. I'm so delighted to know that he is excelling at meeting his goals and enjoying the Life Lab. He comes home with A's and B's and good comments from his teachers.

Trust me, if you let your child explore and try what they want to try, they will AMAZE you! So, don't ignore them or keep them secluded in the house. Enter them into programs like Special Olympics, etc. – there are lots of programs out there. You just have to Google it... Google is a great tool. And search online. There is hope at the end of the tunnel!

My grandmother Louise used to tell me, "Jennifer, put some makeup on, it will make you feel better!" Well, Joshua IS my makeup! He makes me feel better. He makes me feel happy each day! I look at Joshua as my Guardian Angel. He was sent to us for a reason and that was to help me build a good future, a happy one. It was tough, but we made it this far. We are in a very happy place in our lives.

Joshua is improving each day. What more can we ask for? God has been answering all my prayers, and still is.

Jennifer Lee Vegas

And He will continue to answer them if I CONTINUE TO WALK BY FAITH AND NOT BY SIGHT. REMEMBER TO LET GO AND LET GOD!

THANK YOU EVERYONE
WHO HAS BEEN A PART OF OUR LIVES AND
HAS MADE AN IMPACT ON
JOSHUA

ALBERTO PABON, JR., FATHER
MELISSA MALDONADO, SISTER
BIANCA MALDONADO, SISTER
LUIS HERNANDEZ, BROTHER
CESAR CASTRO SR., GRANDFATHER
MARGARET PONZIO-WILLIAMS, GRANDMOTHER
CESAR CASTRO JR., UNCLE
RAMON CASTRO, UNCLE
SANDRA PONZIO-MORGAN, AUNT
MALINA MADRIGAL, AUNT
NICOLE SALAZAR-COGHLAN, AUNT
SERENA HAWKINS, GODMOTHER
SILVIA ORTIZ, AUNT
GINA PABON, GRANDMOTHER
ALBERTO PABON, SR., GRANDFATHER
IVONNE SANTIAGO, FRIEND
CHAZMIN GRANT, FRIEND
SHERRI SADLER, N.P.
DR. BASH
DR. HATHIWALA D., PEDIATRICIAN

DR. ABDELSALAM, PEDIATRICIAN
OPHTHALMOLOGY
CAROLINA RINCON, PHYSICAL THERAPIST
CARMEN CRUZ, M.A., BEHAVIORAL THERAPIST
JENNIFER MONJE, CASE MANAGER
CARMEN ROSA, TEACHER
OSCEOLA SCHOOL DISTRICT
EDGAR CRUZ, PHOTOGRAPHER
AND TO MY HUSBAND, TITO, THANK YOU FOR YOUR SUPPORT THROUGH THIS WHOLE PROCESS; IT WAS A LONG, TOUGH ROAD WRITING THIS BOOK. BUT YOU STOOD RIGHT BY MY SIDE. I LOVE YOU FOREVER! AND LAST BUT NOT LEAST, MY GRANDMOTHER LOUISE, WHO GAVE ME THE INSPIRATION TO WRITE THIS BOOK. THANK YOU, GRANDMA, FOR ALL YOUR STORIES YOU TOLD ME AS A CHILD AND THROUGHOUT THE YEARS. I FINALLY LISTENED TO YOU! THIS BOOK IS DEDICATED TO YOU AND JOSHUA.

WRITTEN BY
<u>JENNIFER LEE VEGAS</u>

www.ingramcontent.com/pod-product-compliance
Lightning Source LLC
Chambersburg PA
CBHW030532080526
44586CB00011B/410